Where the Wind Lives

Where the Wind Lives

Poems From The Great Basin
by Linda Hussa

Linda Hussa (signature)

GIBBS·SMITH
PUBLISHER

SALT LAKE CITY

First Edition

98 97 96 95 94 5 4 3 2 1

This is a Peregrine Smith Book, published by
Gibbs Smith, Publisher
P.O. Box 667
Layton, Utah 84041
(801) 544-9800

Design by Kathleen Timmerman, White Space Design Inferno
Dawn Valentine Hadlock, Editor

Cover Photograph by Linda Dufurrena
Photograph of Linda Hussa by Martin Hoover

Printed and bound in the U.S.A.

Library of Congress Cataloging-in-Publication Data
Hussa, Linda.
Where the wind lives / Linda Hussa.
    p. cm.
ISBN 0-87905-607-X
I. Title.
PS3558.U777W48 1994
811'.54—dc20   94-12402
                                                                    CIP

Acknowledgments

I did not write poetry. I did not hear the music of words.
I was busy seeing the magic of the land and the enchanting lives that
bumped me in this direction, in that. Jean Dunnington slipped a book into
my hand, and then another, and her smiling face said, "Try."

To Lisl Swinehart and Michael Sykes for their goodwill and true hearts.

Thanks also to editors Madge Baird, Lynda Sessions, and most especially,
Dawn Valentine Hadlock. They made a blind journey into a joy.

And to the people of Surprise Valley who let me see into their lives.

Did you forget?
The sky was startling clear.
Only a few stars
bright with heat cooled long before
we held hands here,
before there was such a thing as love.

How can it be seen
long after the passion incinerates,
disperses into vapor?
The physics of it doesn't matter.
There will be this moment
burning brilliant
in some other night.

Contents

Spring *1*

I Am Rain *2*

Lifeguard In The Straw *3*

Orchard In Spring—I *4*

Orchard In Spring—II *5*

I Fix The Fence—The Fence Fixes Me *7*

The Blue Filly *8*

Anniversary Waltz *9*

Homestead In Hell Creek Canyon *10*

Sheepherder *11*

Where The Wind Lives *12*

Nellie *14*

Broken Bowl *16*

Dear Child *17*

The Match *19*

Kick The Can *21*

Horse Runner *22*

Mary *24*

The Cherry Tree *28*

Love Letters *29*

Winter Night In Bruno's—Gerlach, Nevada *30*

Uncle Cicero, My Hero *31*

Homesteaders, Poor And Dry *34*

John Noble's Rye *37*

Nor A Borrower Be *38*

Sewing Circle *40*

One Day Closer To Rain *41*

In This Moment *43*

Mid-Season *44*

Waiting *45*

Jars Of Indian Summer *46*

Under The Hunter Moon *48*

The Barren Mare *49*

The Widow Olson *50*

The End *51*

Storms Of Winter *52*

A Birth *53*

Winter Night *54*

Nevada *55*

Spring

Can it be—
In one night
      ground frost melts away?

Frogs
      one floor down
      in dreams of flies and tadpoles
      feel grassroots tickle
      and push up
      through cold mud
      past worms measuring the meadow
      for robes of Spring.

Frogs
      diviners of gathering water,
      stake claim to a single grass stem,
      fill their throat organs and
      sing

a song composed
      while cold as iron,
      a melody,
      lyric that has a breath of earth alive,
      has the swish of water sliding under ice,
      has a yearning.

The meadow shivers with their jumbled songs.

Sandhill cranes settle like chaff.
A Canada goose rides low on her nest,
      feels the eggs turn inside her.
The rainbow loans out its color
      to buttercups and iris.

Spring must be a woman—
      won't waste her time on flirting
      but gives her all to love.

I Am Rain

I am born among the vapor of wind.
Ever more than one single drop?
I think not.
One drop is enough.
Rounded, clear,
       the reflected eye of God.

From boiling clouds I fall
       pushed by roaring torrents,
       pulled by earth's need
       to the back of a pure white swan
       to cool its thundering body
       as it pierces eternity
       with the tip of a narrow black bill.

Again I fall
       and choose the aspen's weaving branches
       reaching to catch me with shattering leaves,
       holey with wringing prayers.
       I calm their fears.

I slip away
       to fall upon the huddled back of a cottontail
       hovering against the storm.
       Fur dampened, she takes me to her warm skin,
       with a light pink tongue
       she licks me from her paw.

Lifeguard In The Straw

What did I do?
Saved a life
       maybe two
       while China felt the sun
       while the moon
            mooned other lovers
       and solitaire stars
            flashed on the dark fingers of night

The ewe turns, turns
       in the straw jug
       to see what's happening
       behind her

Slurry sagging lamb's head
       under the ewe's tail

I dive in
       push downward through the bloody brine
       where soft hooves prance
       between my fingers
       shy to leave the cozy den

In the nick of time
       two lambs gasp on the straw
       ewe pushing me aside

They've all forgotten me

With bloodied hands
       I walk to the house

The moon slips up
       listening

Orchard In Spring—I

Her garden listens.
Her trees wait
> for warm days to bring her to them
> when they would feel her beneath their branches
> once again.

Rows where the Winesap,
> Bartlett,
> Hale peach
> whisper promises to bees.

Royal Anne hears the tuning up.
Thorny little purple plum
> warms as sap seeps up
> soaking.
> Leaf buds fill with love for blue
> —a color unimagined—
> but where they swell, the limbs
> taste traces of last year's remembrance.

A porcupine
> puts down a foot
> on limber branches,
> pulls back narrow lips
> grasps the bud with his teeth
> and swallows down the sky.

Orchard In Spring–II

Her garden looked up
    through branches of cottonwoods
    at the upstairs window
    with its scalloped light of curtains
    in the midnight sky

    where she folded fabric of a Sunday dress
    well remembered
    against some of his shirts.

The needle pierced them.
White cotton thread bound them.
She could nearly see the quilt top rise
    with his breath,
    her breath
    together.

The dog's bark tore the sweetness,
    drew her to the window
    and where fruit trees stood at random
    in moonlight's sheen
    a dark form
    like a boulder moving
    drew her to anger's height.

Down the stairs
    chair kicked over
    hat,
    coat,
    Winchester by the door
    she flew
    propelled by seven fruit trees girdled
    on their way to dying
    gnawed by this porcupine.

Flashlight axing through the blackness
    searching branches
    and the ground.
    The only sign of the invader
    scarred trees dripping sap
    where he had walked on drifting snow
    and chewed above the stovepipe collars
    laced with wire.

Her trees,
    her beauty trees
    planted in that first year she was married
    —her family
    raised on their fruit

—she
held up
by their smoothly checkered bark,
burst of budding, snow of scent
and bees' humming,
shade of full leaf and rest,
graceful limbs propped to hold the bounty load.

Her trees.

A snapping twig.
In the light
two green eyes glowed from where he slipped bark
on the low fork of the little purple plum.
She stepped forward
put the barrel against the black bristled head
and felt the hooked trigger welcome her finger,
pulled it.
Flame burned the night.
He slumped.
Bark rolled against his teeth.
She shot again,

kicked him from the branches,
shot again
again
again
again
again.

She walked to the house,
stood the rifle by the door,
undressed,
pulled on her flannel gown,
and lay down near enough
to feel her husband's heat.

—*for Bettie Parman*

I Fix The Fence—The Fence Fixes Me

The fence I patched ran away
    rolled a week ahead.
    Ahead.
My horse along for company, we sang
    my horse and me
    Yippie-ti-yi-yo
    so my horse and I would know
    this work—this fence, assigned to me
    was just a lark,
    for I could see
    there were no other ones this free,
    just him and me
    and air
    that danced with Spring
    going in
    and loaded down with dreary Winter
    freed me with each sigh.
    Good-bye.

Fence work is pointed sharp,
    makes me look tight at wire frayed,
    staples sprung, wood posts splayed.
As morning raced on mended wire
    I began to tire
    of all this freedom, and my horse's songs ran dry.
    Spring's snap became a plod,
    the sun burned hot,
    the water gone. I thought of home and company
    then felt the wire
    take a bite of me.
    I looked smaller still to see
    how deep a barb can tear, when
    bluebirds—
    bluebirds, blue as sky
    bluer than a baby's eye
    blue as love's reply—
    flit,
    not fly
    from sage to sage
    on flicker wings, and sing
    Cheer. Cheer lee churn
    each one in turn.

Well—
    what is there for a buckaroo
    to do
    but blush a bit
    at nature's wit
    and blow a kiss
    to birds so blue
    they leave the sky behind.

The Blue Filly

She is just three.
Weaned again.

First time from her dead mother
    small blue head
    in the flank of a still heart.

Second time from a spotted burro
    who let her stand near
    as they swept flies in their head-tail sleep.

Last from the mare band
    that taught her with stinging nips
    to stand back and wait.

She sees him coming.
    Hay poking out in mid-chew
    does she wonder, "What now?"

He speaks her name
    in sound and breath
    she will come to know as her own.

A halter slips over her nose
    and she follows him into the barn
    shivering.

Hobbles hold her
    while the brush sweeps
    firm and soft over her skin.

And when his hand slides down her neck
    I feel it on mine.
    We both relax
    and prepare ourselves for the saddling.

Anniversary Waltz

Let me tell you how it was that day.
She was in the new garden
—she deeded the old one to the morning glory—

·bent, gently touching tender leaves breaking ground.
Shep walked behind her, sitting when she stopped,
his dark dog eyes always on her.

She sowed this garden earlier than most years
before Charlie, her son, could get the springtooth ready.

A noise stopped her. Head tipped listening,
she followed the sound with her clouded eyes
stretching up out of her withered body, taller.

Sandhill cranes. Unmistakable. The courting cantata.
Pearl dust wings flared like capes,
lithe fan dance, coy females,
She listened and saw them in a memory 80 years true.

That afternoon Charlie couldn't find her, running
to search the well house, the attic, the barn,
fearing her heart had failed her in some silent shadow
before he opened the garage and found her Plymouth gone.

The phone was ringing. The Court House.
Charlie took all his questions with him in the truck.
She was on the bench out front,
the spring sun soft on her veiled face,
black and gold-leaf Bible gripped in her gloved hands.

A woman came out, whispered,
> She seems a little confused.
> She's waiting for her husband. He's dead, isn't he?
> She says they're to be married here today.
> You should take her home. Put her to bed.
> Give her some tea. Call the doctor. Poor thing.

They drove home. She did not speak.
Shep ran to meet the truck, put his feet up on the door,
followed her down the hill to the garden,
waited at the gate.

She put her hand on a post,
leaned toward the rusty call of the cranes—sounded once
and flung echoing into the failing light.

Homestead In Hell Creek Canyon

Quiet
Plenty to do
    but

I write Ma again
    —letter pressed with others
    in the lard can
    hidden—

Washing's hung out
    dry
    'fore it's pinned
    wood stacked neat by the stove
    bread loaves
    sweet smell
    and steam
    browned just like
    Mister
    likes 'em

Floor is sprinkled down
    washed my feet
    hair's braided
    up, forget-me-nots tucked in
    rubbed my hands with sheep's grease
    that tramp herder gave me
    Mister hates the smell, but they're awful cracked

Brought the cow up from the willows
    she's slow walkin'
    but I don't mind
    in the lean-to shade
    my cheek on her flank, I squeeze those big finger tits
    the warmth of her
    stomach workin'

I hear Mister comin'
    pull foolish flowers from my braids
    hold them behind my skirts
    until he's gone by
    he nods
    I nod back
    milk spills
    white drops slide between my toes

The cow leaves the shed
split hoof
tiny blue petals
in the same track

Sheepherder

Basco boy, you
    left your sheep bedded
    walked the many ridges
    through a dark where lightning warned you back

    to stand outside the homesteader cabin in the rain
    until he found you
    took you inside where you sat on the floor
    shivering
    and watched the young girl they called teacher
    move like a dance

    and speak to his children in their language
    you didn't understand

    but her voice was enough.

The man put you out at last
closed the door on her eyes.

You found the flock still bedded near your dogs

and for days
and nights
you heard her voice say,
"Good night,
            basco boy."

Where The Wind Lives

The Paiute woman looked out the car window and indicated the deep, turn-ing canyon with her chin. "That is where the wind lives," she said. After a pause she added, "Of course, white people don't believe that."

Alone with the desert—
    the wind and me.
Silent together and contented so.
I seek the salve of this place
    for wounds too deep to bind,
    for sorrows that bleed my soul.

I have left my horse behind,
    still I am the tallest thing.
    I can be seen and heard.

My tracks mar smooth sand.
I try to step from rock to rock
    denying my own passage
    but I tire of the deception,
    step down,
    and leave my print behind.

The sage grows grey and taut
    ignoring its thirst.
Beneath the brush
    here and there
    miniature plants bloom.
    Flowers the size of flies' eyes
    see me pass
    and I see them.

I walk toward a draw where I know a spring to be.
I am a dowsing rod drawn to the water
    and it drips off my chin.
Its flow an impossible secret.
Here the sage grows greedy,
    thicker in the waist and taller than I.
Grass so plump with water I could wring it.
If I sat quietly
    I could match cast tracks to their makers,
    but I did not come to observe those of heart and breath.

Above the spring
    a canyon runs deep and sharp
    filled with discontented shrubs
    wanting to feel each passerby.

It is in this dark gash
    of orange lichen rocks
    the Paiutes say
    the wind lives.

I know how it roams the desert alone,
    feeling the tickle of the sage on its belly,
    shivering aspen leaves,
    rifting the sand to dance,
    taking on it scents and sounds that are not its own.

This marriage place of wind with earth,
    longing to be one against the other,
    bodies moving
    in the eternal caress,
    but nearness is all that can be theirs.

But I want to see the wind alone.
I go higher
    to the place of the emergence.

I stand on the rim,
    lift my arms
    to the wind.
    Ashes of the dead pull from me,
    rasp my eyes,
    stain my skin with holy dust.

Is the sigh mine
    or its own?

Nellie

Nellie worked for the white woman
    in the ranch house standing
    exactly where she saw her first antelope
    beside the aspens
    where named roses were planted in rows.
The antelope with soft eyes
    looking at her.
    She
    a baby playing—
    while her mother gathered wormwood and nettle—
    looked back at him.
Now she wondered
    if the antelope was a young man on a vision quest
    or a spirit returned with a message.

The woman said "Nellie!" in a sharp voice.

Nellie took her eyes off the memory
    and followed the brush making circles on the floor.
When dinnertime came she took her plate of food
    outside
    under the trees
    alone.
It began with a table full of working men
    and no empty chair for Nellie.
    And it was never changed.

Nellie walked her life from one-room government housing
    to that house
    with the rose garden
    and gatherings of white people.
    Her babies knew the work
    —tied to her back
    or propped in the cradleboard
    she sewed of deerskin smoked ivory,
    beads traded for—everything—
    sewn on for beauty.
She made gloves and purses
    for the white woman who paid hard money
    for the novelties.

The house became cracked and woody, like the roses.
On a day the men were away tending cattle on the desert
      the woman held hard to the edge of Nellie's plate.
      "Take your dinner with me, Nellie."

      Nellie looked into the blue eyes.
      She pulled slowly away from the gripping fingers,
      and went out
      where the antelope
      stood with her all those years.

—in memory of Nellie Townsend

Broken Bowl

A Paiute woman sat here on this sand
    where cattails of worn brown velvet
    spawned the steamy air of Hot Springs Valley.

    She ground pine nuts
    gathered with the mountain's blessing
    in this lava bowl

    that struck against my horse's hoof
    and led me like a reed whistle calling widgeon in.

Sand glitters against my eyes,
    but I know the rhythm of her body.
    I hear the rock chewing seeds.
    I smell the pierce of sage where
    the magpie grips it watching.

Was the bowl given down

    or did her man travel
    to the distant caldera,
    search out a lava shape to serve

and she, in ignorance of time walking toward her
    began to chip,
    heated the rock in a greasewood fire,
    let water beads popping
    fracture flakes,
    mere flakes,
    then chip and grind to form the bowl?

No gentle cove of sand could web her wandering
    —children strapped to the clutch of women
    behind the men—
    shoulders hunched toward game or harvest.

Left buried in the sand
    heavy stone tools—metate, mano, mortar, pestle—
    of a woman common among her tribe

    until cold winds drove them back to warm mists rising
    where dunes drifted in curving lines repeated.

Over this bowl she bent as grasses' heavy heads of seed
    and felt the scrape of stone against her bones.

Dear Child

We gathered the desert in June
    to brand calves born since turn-out
    to move them up to the mountain
        with the feed.

June is hot on the desert.
Days are long on the desert.

Ride a wide circle,
    gather toward a gate,
        brand the afternoon away,
            trot to camp
              and supper
                and bed.

I worried about Katie,
    our tiny girl of seven,
But she pushed Smokey near a rock,
    shinnied up his old leg
        and rode out among the buckaroos.

The sun came out hot
    as Katie and I rode across Butcher Flat,
    swung toward Sarvis
        pushing cattle in front of us.
I sent her to the ridges
    into sudden draws
        for a break from the pecking along behind.
Always, some small calves
    keeping up,
        little hocks brushing,
        tails swinging,
            on the long trail
            to be branded.

In the early afternoon
    we saw the rest bunched
        through the dust choking us
        and heat waves dancing,
        smoke drifting hotter,
            the branding started.

Katie croaked, "I'm thirsty."
"I know."
      But it was in my
      Words-of-wisdom period
      and I said,
            "There's no use complaining, dear child.
                  We're all thirsty
                  and we're all hungry
                  and we're all tired.
            We have to finish the work.
            When the work is done
                  we can rest.
            You don't hear anyone else say,
                  'I'm thirsty.'
            They all are
                  but they don't say it.
                        Saying it makes us all twice as thirsty.
            Hold on, we'll be there soon."

We finished the day.
Trotting back to camp
      Katie was strong in the middle,
            learning how buckaroos only tease those they like.

She had a water fight in the spring before supper,
      ate like a field hand,
      fell asleep sitting up.

When I tucked her into the bedroll
      I kissed her sunburned cheeks and said,
            "You were perfect today."
And in her own child's wisdom she said,
      "No, Mom. Not perfect
            . . . almost perfect."

One day soon
      to her small boy
            she'll say,
                  "There's no use complaining,
                                    dear child."

The Match

Through a child's eyes
    I see twilight on the desert
    slanting light finds cracks in the clouds
    and warms the meadow
    with the heart's golden blood.
Not yet dark.
Not still day.

Dinner waits on the table steaming
    and I am sent to fetch the men.

Down the meadow
    I follow the path worn by hooves
    to the pasture
    where they've gone to turn their horses,
    my father and his brother.

Around the bend I hear dark, rough sounds
    and go forward slowly
    half afraid,
    half cautious,
    all curious.
Low on the meadow
    my men are fighting.
    They thrust their bodies forward
    boots tearing into the sod,
    spurs thrown aside,
    hats tumble from sweaty heads
    and are crushed beneath them as they churn
    while combat draws gasps and grunts
    and they grapple in the fading light
    of their youth.

I sink behind a brush
    scared and sick
    they would break a rule
    made for my brother and me.

At last they struggled to their feet
    and came toward me,
    each an arm around the other.
    Dad's white shirt
    Mom had carefully ironed that morning
    while he stood in his Levis and bare chest
    drinking his coffee
    and teasing her
    was torn,
    stained with grass, dirt,
    and splashed with blood,
    his and his brother's.

I drew back knowing
    with blood flowed anger,
    but they came laughing,
    unevenly swaggering toward me.

Then one turned and ran back
    for their hats and spurs.
    Joined again with arms on arms,
    hats cocked off center,
    one smeared blood with the back of his hand
    and they laughed again.

In their innocence
    and I in mine
    I stand as they come toward me.

I see a trickle of red from Dad's nose,
    a curl of damp hair on his temple,
    their faces happy,
    and I know there is a kind of love
    my brother and I have not discovered.

—*for L. D. Vinson,*
in memory of Lee Vinson

Kick The Can

Music of a child's night game
    plays on shadowed grass
    beneath the yard light.
Parents listen from the house
    to squeals as children run and hide
    from the one who's
    "it."

Beyond the fettered light
    in plumes of spring's sweet essence
    shadows half breathe
    and when it's safe to—giggle.

Swift dark shadows slip
    from bush and tree trunk
    to kick the can and set all the prisoners free.

The "it" one steps in barefoot silence
    from the spotlight
    stares at black on black,
    listening for a heart's whisper
    hears instead
    curlews cry
    from the meadow, "Run!"

Horse Runner

He rides in darkness folding 'round.
The ring of hoof on desert floor
    ricochets off the moon.
He hears each twice
    and looks to see behind.
He is alone.
    He only feels another's flesh.

On the desert edge of uncharted dunes
    trails bleed
    toward the springheart of the Buffalo Hills.
Fox- or ferret-like and belly down
    that is where he finds them feeding.

The scent of horses fills him.
The stallion sleeps standing.
The lead mare stares him eye to eye
    then throws a warning in the dawning air.

The run begins. He lets them have it,
    mounts his blood bay slow and follows in a trot.
Their dust—the target—
    by evening barely lifting wisps.
    Footsore and thirsty
    far off their home ground
    they've given up escape.

He was a horseman.
    Horses taught him.
    Horses fought him.
    Horses made him whole.
    At times, they were his only friend
    gave him legs and mind
    to catch their own.

He drove them through the tall pole gate
    of the compound.
A woman on the porch
    pulled a hat on her brown hair
    walked by rows and rows of wire kennels
    where German Shepherds
    leaned against the wire like hopeful prisoners
    whining as she passed.

In the round corral
    the best were sorted. The others put off alone.
Greenbacks folded in jeans pocket
    with thanks he didn't hear,
    meal refused, he rode out past the dogs
    and saw horses galloping hard
    disappear in the jangle of the wire.

Behind, the shooting started.
He stabbed his spurs
    into the fine hide
    of the blood bay
    but he could not ride faster than the speed of sound.

Mary

They said she lived "out East"
four days by a wagon,
one day on a fast horse
if death was on the way.
The women called her Mary,
the men said "Sweet Marie,"
but only in their secret thoughts
in the loneliness of night
as they recalled how she would ride
in the manner of a man
with laughing eyes and chestnut hair
and a face that filled their dreams
on a leggy pinto gelding,
too snuffy for a woman,
she was a shadow in the saddle
without a thought of perils ahead.

When the men who shared the open range
branded up their cattle
Mary'd stack her dallies smokin',
turn her horse and ride away.
The critter she had lassed
behind her horse came draggin'
as she rode toward the fire
and the branding iron's sear.
She used a long reata
made for her just special
by a man who tried to woo her
but had too long been a friend.

She knew the mountains and the canyons
the big wide open grasslands.
She knew the desert country
like the inside of her heart.
She lived out in the rocky breaks
on the south side of the mountain,
in the winter when her cattle
rustled feed among the sage.
In the summer she moved higher,
to a grassy, high-walled canyon
where, as a prisoner to the silence,
the life she'd chosen locked her in.

Those men who used the desert
took an interest in this woman.
They helped her brand her cattle.
She helped them gather strays.
They helped her when her parents died
of flu in nineteen eighteen.

She helped them run their horses.
They helped her put up hay.
They brought her sacks of nutmeats
and little sacks of raisins,
as precious as gold nuggets,
she baked up in a cake
as they sat outside her cabin
in the shade of golden aspens
and when the fall work was completed
rolled their beds and rode away.
And when the winter blew in cold,
and they were snug back in the home place,
she'd be alone out on the desert,
in her rock cabin in the breaks.

One open winter she surprised them
and rode to town for Christmas.
She visited 'round the valley,
brought them gifts that she had made.
For the dance, she wore a velvet dress,
the color of the redbud,
the first sign spring was coming,
and that's how she made them feel.
There she met a man named Hayden
who led her to the dance floor
and though she rode and roped as men did,
she was a woman in his arms.
To the soft strains of Blue Danube
Mary followed where he led her.
She gazed up at him, but not shyly,
with a smile no man had seen.

In the spring, when grass had started
the men trotted down to Mary's
to have a cup of coffee
and bring her up to date,
but who stepped from the cabin,
the young buck known as Hayden.
The men all sat their horses
until Mary came outside.
Well, she gave a whoop and holler
and pulled them from their saddles,
then smiling up at Hayden asked,
"Who'll be first to kiss the bride?"

When they gathered up their feelings
they pulled home brew from their pockets
and tried their best to let go
of their love for Sweet Marie.

The desert lovers worked together
riding early in the morning
when the sunlight chases shadows
and the larks sing on the sage
and the air is scented heavy
horses trot along together,
stirrups touch, and then the hands do,
spreading warmth up to the heart.

It was in the fall the next year,
prices dropped, the cowman suffered.
Belts were tightened 'til it choked them—
Mary and Hayden felt the pinch.
Her little bunch of cattle
were enough for beans and bacon,
she could live on next to nothing,
but with two, they needed more.
So, Hayden borrowed a little money
from a banker in the valley,
but when things were turning sour,
the bank began to make demands.
Sleepless nights followed daydreams
of losing horses, cows and homestead,
moving from her precious desert
where she had taken her first breath.

Mary saddled up her pinto
and rode up through the canyon
to the crest of the mountain
and looked across the land.
The land that she called mother,
the land that she called friend,
the land she chose for life,
that drank the tears she cried alone.
But this love she found with Hayden,
that made the desert fuller,
gave her something far more precious
than horses, cows or home.
And so she vowed to tell him
that a tent, or raft, or lean-to,
would be home as long as they were
side by side and heart by hand.

Down a finger of the canyon
the drift of calves a'bawling came
up to Mary where she was riding,
so she turned her horse that way.
Expecting one, there was a dozen,
calves unbranded, inside a fence.

Mary knew someone was rustling.
Who it was, she could not guess.
She turned her horse to go get Hayden
but noticed tracks along the trail
and felt an ice hand hold her heart still.
The tracks were going to beat her home.

That night at supper he laughed as always.
They washed the dishes and from their bed
watched the moon rise full and golden.
The aspens' quaking was inside of her.
She drew his arm across her breast
like a blanket and held it near,
to keep the night's chill from her body,
but couldn't keep it from her heart.

The moonlight on the bed clothes
shone on his face contented.
Nothing there to cry out *Rustler!*
Nothing but the man she loved.
Yet his conscience seemed unburdened.
He had stolen from her friends,
things they would gladly give him,
if he had only asked for help.
Was his love of higher value
than honor to her friends?
And what of lonely days before her
on this land without her man?

When she tried to leave her bedside
his arms went round her, pulled her tight.
Held her body close up to him
closer, closer man and wife.

While the stars winked in the midnight
she rode the pinto up the trail,
drove the calves out of the canyon,
and watched them scatter through the sage.

The gelding moved to take the trail home,
to her canyon, to her man,
but she checked him, and she turned him
to the trail along the crest.

As she went far from the desert
sunlight broke across the land,
golden flow chasing shadows,
and the lark sang on the sage.
All her life, she recalled that morning
and her heart wept every time,
for the loves she left behind,
where the lark sings on the sage.

The Cherry Tree

Halfway down the field it grew
    along the ditch bank
    where it stooped to drink
    as summer dried the roots
    and made them tingle.

Halfway down the field it blossomed
    cherry pink and white.
    Wild bees and I could see it from faraway
    and we buzzed toward it.

It was high and from the branches hidden
    I could see farther than the moon,
    farther than the inside of me.

One day it was gone,
    just plain gone.
Men—a father and a pushy hired man
    too lazy to break a wheel line on the tree's set
    chainsawed it down
    as if it was an enemy,
    or a horse thief,
    and left the charred trunk in ashes smoldering.

    —You know how men are about progress.

My tree is cut,
    limbs stacked in the woodshed.
    We put everything to use—brains, innards, blood—
    everything,
    but I'll be damned
    if anyone
    is going to burn
    one stick of my cherry tree.

Love Letters

"Wow!" was written in the dust
    on the bedside table.

The dawn and I blushed together
    as your spurs
    ching
    chinged
    around the kitchen
    and you started the fire.

I stretched full length
    on the cool smoothness
    of the sheets,

a kept woman
    a moment longer.

Within an hour's time
    we'll be ahorseback
    in a long trot
    to some distant blue mountain
    hunting cows.

I'll carry your message
    close
    knowing there will come a day
I would give a year of my life
    for that . . .
        "Wow!"

Winter Night In Bruno's—Gerlach, Nevada

She watches the door open,
    cold wind and snow
    swirl around boots.

Just a glance
    to see if he's alone
    then boldly tracking the mirrored image above the bar
    as if it's one-way
    and her eyes can't be felt
    tiptoeing around him.

She has a thing for cowboys—
    can't ride one side of a horse—
    but she's lost in her Roy Rogers crush
    hoping Trigger is tied outside
    and Dale is home with Buttermilk.

What she doesn't see in the mirror
    is her own desperation showing.
    She wears it like dangling earrings
    a sharp flash through her long hair when the light is right.

Her voice is soft
    and opens in
    fascinating, the easy way her body moves on the stool
    cigarette for company,
    dancing, pressed against whoever,
    an intimacy allowed a stranger
    she wouldn't nod to in passing
    while she waits for her cowboy.

No bar banter reaches her. She is alone.
    Blue neon reflects on her face.
    The glow of a dandelion under a child's chin
    means they love butter.
    What is the blue thing she loves?

She could catch a ride to Reno—maybe.
    But she's done that before,
    running through the sand dunes,
    car door open,
    guy's face in the dash lights
    calling, 'Hey baby, I didn't mean nothin'.'

It was a long, scary walk back home
    and she's not there yet.

Uncle Cicero, My Hero

Aunt Josie was a disagreeable woman.
    Something cut happiness from her hide
    and left a scar that was her smile.
She wasn't exactly mean
    just every word that came out,
    every look,
    slid into you like a spider bite
    and humped up your skin
    and irritated you all day.
We all just plain felt sorry for Uncle Cicero
    'cause he had to live with her.
    He musta had spider welts all over his body.

She had a voice like a pig gettin' its ears pulled.
    Oh, she'd try to be nice
    but that's just it,
    she'd have to try
    and when she did it would set your teeth on edge.

She collared me once
    and took me on a picture tour through their house.
    They not only had separate beds
    they had separate rooms
    and I remember wondering what occasion would happen
    to get them in the same bed.
    Halley's Comet?

Uncle Cicero was one of those old-fashioned men
    who put his necktie on
    before he got out of bed.
    Always wore a dark suit
    with the gold chain of his Elgin watch
    holding in his front.
He was a railroad man
    and you can't be one
    unless you've got a watch
    and are devoted to it.

To say Aunt Josie was bossy
    is like saying a mule will stick.
    She had the house in her name,
    the car in her name,
    the telephone in her name
    because she came with some piddling dowry
    and he had nothing but himself
    which meant a man not afraid to work,
    a good head and heart
    as dependable as his watch
    and somehow
    when you saw him comin'
    you always smiled.

Aunt Josie won the county spelling bee
        three years in a row
        so she figured herself a genius
        and Uncle Cicero did nothing to unconvince her.

Nothing gave him greater pleasure
        besides playing the fiddle
        than handing over his paycheck
        every Friday of the world
        and having her dole out 50 cents a day for incidentals.
        She figured he couldn't get plastered on 50 cents
        but she was wrong—
        all he had to do is stop by one of the 18 bars in town
        Saturday afternoon
        and play his fiddle for drinks.
        It was for this reason I took up the fiddle.

He never did anything untoward.
        Nothing that got talked about anyway—
        unless you counted the Widow Charles.

Mrs. Charles was left alone
        while still in her travelin' days.
We didn't know the ages of adults back then.
        If they gave up keeping pollywogs trapped in fruit jars
        they were old.
Anyway, Mrs. Charles wasn't SO old.
        She took to rouging her cheeks
        3 or 4 years after Mr. Charles fell out of the apple tree
        on his head.
One Sunday Momma sent me over to visit
        while she went off to a church doin's.
        Uncle Cicero and I were in the basement
        workin' on his model railroad.
        It was a wonderful thing
        even though I was gettin' too old for playing with trains
        and kids my age didn't have hobbies.
        They just hung around
        'til they were old enough to buy a junker pickup,
        then they were a man.

Aunt Josie was fryin' chicken upstairs.
        I could smell it.

Uncle Cicero checked his Elgin,
        walked over to the wall and flipped a switch.
        Then he filled two glasses with hard cider,
        handed one to me, and
        leaned back against his workbench.
We saluted each other
        and I let the cider put the clamps on my tongue.
        In a few minutes

Aunt Josie called down the stairs to Uncle Cicero.
  There wasn't any water.
No water, he said.
  It must be that darned pump again.
  He never cussed in front of women.
Well, she said
  she was fixin' supper and NEEDED some WATER.
Okay, he said
  he'd get her some,
  picked up a pail
  and motioned me to come on.
I hated to leave that cider,
  and the smell of the chicken frying,
  and the coolness of the basement,
  but I went along
  so's I wouldn't get trapped by the spider woman.
Uncle Cicero headed like a bee straight
  for the Widow Charles' house.
  She met him at the door
  in a dress even I knew was
  attractive.
It was so strange
  because it was like she knew we were coming.
  She invited us in to her kitchen.
  There was a pitcher of lemonade on the table
  with ice.
We sat down and they commenced to visiting
  like old friends catching up.
  There were lots of funny stories and laughin'.
  After a while
  she carried his pail to the sink and filled it up.
  She handed it to him and saw us to the door.
  I can still see her standing in the shadows
  watchin' us go.
Uncle Cicero set the pail in the sink
  and told Aunt Josie he'd go work on the pump.
  And she said, don't get greasy
  'cause supper was about ready.

Uncle Cicero pulled his chair up to the pump
  poured us another glass of cider and sat down.
  Every once in a while he'd whack the pump with a wrench.
When we finished our cider
  he got up,
  walked over to the switch,
  flipped it on,
  and the pump started up, humming.
THERE, he called up the stairs.
  FIXED IT. Now, you've got water, Josie.
Then we went upstairs for supper.

Homesteaders, Poor And Dry

The world was bone dry.
I don't know why God would do such a thing.
The field was bare as the floor
And the springs nothin'—nothin'.

Papa's cattle bawled night and day
  'til I thought I'd go crazy with it.
  Turn them out, I cried.
  Kill them, Papa, I begged.
  And he did.
  And he killed himself, too
  in a way
  'cause he loved them crazy ol' cows.
I had to help him.
There wasn't anybody else.
  Momma had the baby.

He handed me the big knife
  and I followed him.
First he took the red one,
  the one he didn't like the most.
  Old Mule, he called her 'cause she kicked him every day.
He coaxed her into the barn.
She went hoping for some hay.
the barn still smelled like hay,
  so she went.
He tied her up
  and took the knife from me
  held it 'round behind his back
  He thought she'd know what he was up to,
  and run.
He slipped his arm around her neck
  and the knife came up
  sharp and glinting
  like a present.
His hands were shaking.
He had killed cows and pigs and chickens
  millions of 'em
  but his hands were shaking now.
This dry had him half crazy too.
Just when I thought he wouldn't do it
  he screamed
  and I screamed
  and old Mule screamed.

She pulled back
and her wild eyes looked right at me.
Blood thumped out of her and she fell
shaking the ground under me
as if I was going, too.

Papa was on his knees crying,
    I'm sorry, old Mule, I'm sorry,
    and I ran away.
I threw the gate open
    and chased the other cows away.
    I didn't know where they'd go,
    but somebody else could kill 'em.
    Not my Papa.

The next week the well went dry.
Papa would drop the bucket down
    and it would come up empty.
He turned the bucket over and the bottom was wet.
He said I'd have to go down in the well
    and fill the bucket
    with a cup.
    I'd have to
    'cause we could never pull him up.
    He was the strongest
    and the well was small
    and I was the smallest.
    No Papa. I can't.
    Yes, you can, girl. You can do it for the baby.
He tied a stick in the rope
    for me to stand on
    and boosted me over the side.
    I could only see a few feet down
    then there was a black hole
    and I was looking into the belly of a monster.
    A monster that would take me in one swallow
    and I didn't even get to have my own baby and home yet.
    His face brushed mine
    and I whispered, No Papa.
    No.
    But the rope was sliding down over the edge
    and I was going down too.
I clung onto that rope
    nothing could get me loose.

There were things down there.
Scary things that would touch me.
Papa's face in the circle of sky went farther away
until I couldn't see him
only a black circle in a blue circle
getting smaller.
The well was so narrow
the walls brushed me.

It was dark
and places big rocks stuck out and scraped me.
I cried let me up
let me up
but I was still going down,
leaving the world
leaving Mama crying my name
and my Papa moaning, it's for the baby, girl.

I was lowered down in that well every day
'til the drought broke.
Every day.
I closed my eyes and sang myself songs,
dipped the water raising down there in the pitch dark
all by the feel.
But there was no time I'll remember
like that first time.
After, when the water came back up in the well,
I went and looked down into the water
and imagined myself on the bottom
and sometimes I wanted to go back down
to the quiet of the dark.

In all my life
Nothing can make me scared.
I went down into the earth
and drew back up.
Nothing can ever scare me again.
No man.
No beast.
No God.
I seen His face that day
and He promised me
no fear.

John Noble's Rye

There's this field, see,
    right next to ours—
    only the barbed-wire fence between.
    Our side subs—timothy, clover, a pretty meadow.
John Noble's side is dry.
No spring.
No water right.

Every fall he is out there on that rusted tractor
    farming that dry field in straight, smooth passes,
    like his wife sweeping up before the pastor calls.
    I can see his dust from our place.

He drills golden flakes of hardy rye in the grey dirt,
    the packers behind are his long fingers
    patting down the seed for winter.
Some years it comes up and stops. A green haze,
    no more, and he turns his cows in for what they can get.
But this year he hit the storms, Bullseye!
The rye came thick with heads like wheat
    up to the saddle skirts.
They're talking about John Noble's rye in town.

Bobby will be home from his job in the city soon.
    He'll wake in his upstairs room with the cowboy wallpaper
    —his barefeet on the narrow stairs, John Noble waiting
    in the kitchen—and know why he comes back.

The two of them will lead the sorrel mare into the field
    every dawn
    and when she nips the heads

    they'll make hay.

Nor A Borrower Be

New pickup, shiny, clean pulls into the yard
    No hay stacked three tiers high
    No jumper cables or fix-it-all tool box
        or handyman jack
        or wads of baling wire
        or cans of staples
        or hammer with pipe handle welded on
        or fork or shovel
        or pile of rusted chains
    No 30.30 resting between dining-out coyotes
    No old dog on the seat along for the ride.

A new pickup with three men inside
    shoulder to shoulder
    stiff clothes with ironed creases
    stiff faces with importance.

Walking out to meet them
    a man in worn clothes that know sweat, not starch
    rough hand
        that sends a loop surely
        pulls a colt sweetly
        seals a deal
        changes a wheel
        and bleeds
    is extended politely
    to men
        who won't meet his eyes.

Inside, the woman
    sets out cream and sugar and cups for coffee
    as if in welcome.

Banker's eyes that see past people
     to the bottom line
     dissect her books with retractable scalpels
     ask for supporting documents she cannot find
     shame her ignorant, high school concepts
          disappearing cash flow
          five-year projections
          unrealistic budget
     as if
          the six-year drought
          rising costs
          doubling taxes
          market downturns
          found their origin somewhere in this house.

The brutal silence of retribution
     of computer models projecting failure to pay
     sell down or else
     as years of work wadded up in pages of red ink.

And when those men are gone
     two stone people
     in bitter silence
     the hurt so deep
     there is no solace
     in each other's arms.

Sewing Circle

Use the long curving needle
    better for speed and it's sharp.
Start with a slip stitch
    no need to sew blind, simply sew it
    and gentle, be gentle.

Pull soft where the pieces are missing
    time will fill in the rest.
Begin and just sew,
    it's slippery, I know. Quickly,
    work quickly, work fast.

"Old Ned? (Lapper, Spot, Sox, Little Bess)
    Why, he was curled by the fire
    my slippers under his chin
    his running dreams made the children laugh
    never hurt a fly, that one."

My evening by the flashlight's fire
    quilting bloody flaps,
    pushing puckers out into a whole sheep.

Five little town dogs, crazed by sport
    follow a full moon through meadows
    pack of shadows slide along
    where the flock is bedded
    until they woke to a low wail,
    and yip.
    We woke to their pain.

Twenty-seven little sheep, dazed by death
    strewn, whimpering
    —sheep whimper when hurt, like us—
    three floating in the pond, one gutted
    fine white wool dyed a vomitus shade of red.

We sewed them, skinned faces
    jaws flapping, legs waving
    our anger seared by the work.

So, you say it wasn't old Ned (Blackie,
    Irish, Tommy or Princess).
    I stood under the porch light
    and handed over his collar
    —strands of bloody wool in the catch.

One Day Closer To Rain

Dry land
    plants, grasses, clover dehydrated
    crunch underfoot
    like crackers.

No green left
    only bitter gold.
    Every bit of moisture
    is drawn down to sustain life.

Rich peat
    is faded and powdery.

In many places
    dirt is all you see.

Cracks appeared in August
    wider and deeper now—
    the earth's skin is wounded,
    dying.

I've given up checking the news
    yet refuse the notion
    this is a trend.

I am a rancher so,
    though I don't measure the wings of the crooked beetle,
    or count cricket chirps at sundown,
    I hope
    for rain.

But when thunderheads gather,
    black in the belly,
    a veil of rain drying midair,
I ignore it as I would a fickle lover
    who has strayed,
    tests his chance for return,
    and I ache in secret.

Where artesians flowed
    pipes stand rust red,
    the darkness of routing returns my own anxious breath
    a dry echo.

Meadows, where water stood and snipes waded,
    are parched sedges.
    Even they are breaking down.

The playa, once a luminous reflection of soft blue sky,
    is an arid flat
    blistered and broken into a Picasso puzzle
    of geometric tiles.

And in the afternoon
      dust rises on the wind
      and is suspended,
      too light to fall.

Deep trails lead cattle from the cold desert
      over the eastern rims.
      They come home
      not knowing
      it is the same here.

Don't we remember
      the world was perfect
      when we were young?
      If not perfect,
      dependable?
      And if not the world,
      the weather?

We fall back on faith
      when there is nothing we can do
      but pray.

In This Moment

I felt the blow
    somewhere inside that is heart and chest
    being and feeling
    and knowing

    knowing

    the sound
    the jerk that came together.

My mare danced on four legs.
    She could not move on three.

Hoof held dangling
    muscles cramping
    eyes that clouded
    as mine closed
    on this moment laid hard against
    one so clear.

The walk away
    for the rifle
    thirty-aught-six
    aught—ought—ought not.

I hold the mechanics of shiny brass
    and rifling true
    the breech
    the bolt.

Marksmanship is wasted
    when the barrel fits the ear

    and she is blown
    into my memory
    where she will dance.

Mid-Season

This piece of time
    between summer and fall
    asks for its own name.

There is no morning heat
    and yet no fingering frost at night.

Geese move up from the lake before dawn
    and back down as the moon lifts.
    They stir but do not leave.
    The garden slows.
    Hornets begin their grey paper nests in the branches
    hurrying.

This body of no season
    pushes against mine
    and makes me smile.

It might be best left unnamed
    free of expectation
    to just appear

    a cape
    wrapping magic.

Waiting

Beside the table sitting
the ivy has a new leaf since yesterday
when she sat there
in the heartbreaking silence.

The jay is standing in the seed box
kicking like an old hen hunting worms.
She should take her Daisy BB gun
     and pop him in the britches
but doesn't move
because she's waiting.

Fifty odd years of marriage
taught her to wait
for his return,
for the rattley noise his truck made
     from the half mile away
     down the canyon.
Even the old black dog recognized it.
He would get up out of the dust,
     stretch,
     walk out,
     yawn,
     and sit down to wait.

She waited for the last word on his daily itinerary
     and made her plans then.
It was a partnership
     with him the major stockholder.

She silently steered his life,
     a deep strong current
     the ship had no power against,
     taking him across latitudes not on his charts.
She waited with him for the doctor
     then she helped him wait to die.

Now she must undo that thing inside her
     that tells her to wait.

Jars Of Indian Summer

Down dark cellar stairs
    Wild Plum jam—
    jars of an afternoon on the mountain

    between haying and gathering,
    between wishing school would start
    and that crazy loneliness when it finally does.

Wild plums,
    ruby skin,
    bitter fruit of tormented root
    sugaring
    when frost settles on a sleeping dog.

We traded plums
    for silly jokes and laughter
    draped on limbs
    to keep the bushes through the long white winter silence.
    Deer nibble bare purple branches
    and taste our being there.

A lump of porcupine baby
    balanced on thin branches
    ate his share.

The kids chased trout
    through stained glass water
    splashing voices in the air.

A discovery echoed through the canyon
    a narrow trail
    a righteous out house
    open door in welcome
    yellowed calendar
    1937 lady with shining hair.
    So many years alone—
    each kid stepped in
    and closed the door.

We burst through Grandma's back door
    into her white kitchen
    and soap opera sorrows
    with buckets and boxes of plums
    and stories to tell
    crowding close.

She showed how to cut out the pits,
    poured white sugar mountains
    and cooked our day into jam.

On a Sunday morning
    I held a jar in my hand.
    The ruby beauty
    thick with sunlight.

They took it from me,
    put it back on the shelf
    and closed the door.

—for Katherine Hussa

Under The Hunter Moon

I slip the rifle sling over my shoulder
    and step into the silence of dawn
Geese move through the darkened sky
    toward the pond
    wings cut the quiet
    with an oddly mechanical sound
    and then their voices set me right

I open the gate
    and the sheep rise from their beds
    as if I commanded it so
Lambs rush to thump flanks for milk
    kept warm through the autumn night

I fall in with their march up the meadow
    to find clover that grew while they slept
Stalks of blue chicory and tiny golden trefoil
    fold inside pink lips, and chewing
    they walk on

At the fence line I know the place
    where soft pads left prints in the dust
    by a hole in the woven wire
    and I am a warrior hunched in rose briars
    their scent pale, and their thorns pick at my wool coat

Stern in my resolve
    I wait while the sun creeps to the edge of the day
Slain lambs, guts ripped open
Magpies and blowflies
Blaating ewes with swollen bags searching the flock

A lamb a day for two weeks
    I grip the rifle tighter

A shadow comes toward me through the moonlight
    grey and tan, she arches in a mouse pounce
    and works her way toward the barrel of my rifle
    toward the bullet I will hurl
    at her heart

I watch her snatch mice out of the grass
    flip them up like popcorn
    down the hatch. She is a comic
    this coyote, playing, laughing
    making her way steadily toward me
    my finger soft on the cold steel trigger

Coyote stops
    looks directly at me
Her eyes hold me accountable

The Barren Mare

Filly foal
    not considered
    for a saddle horse.
No mares allowed
    they cause trouble with the geldings.
Brood mare band
    in her third year.

Next spring
    no foal.

One more chance
    'cause she's strong
    good bone
    straight
    good back.

Next spring
    no foal.
Call the killers.

What chance
    does a woman have
    in a world like that?

The Widow Olson

So we passed this neat little ranch
    on the edge of Catlow Valley.
A perfect community of outbuildings
    held apart by government issue poplars and cottonwoods.

"Whose place is that?"
    I asked the old buckaroo beside me.

He thought back to a winter ride
    when a teenage wrangle boy drove a herd of horses
    one hundred blue miles
    measuring each day by the homestead trees in the distance.

"The Widow Olson lives there.
    At least she used to.
    Her husband died
    and she ran the place after that."

His eyes of half Chinese,
    half Paiute,
    inscrutable to the second power
    looked into mine.

I imagined a single woman
    120 miles from town,
    a day's ride from the nearest neighbor,
    riding, working, living
    alone
    alone
    alone.

"How long did she run the place
    alone?"
    alone
    alone

"Oh," he thought back to her kitchen
    and the food on his plate,
    and the stove by his bed glowing red
    and her soaking up the silence of the boy,
    "30 or 40 years."

"A woman ran a ranch out here
    for 30 or 40 years
    ALONE
    and you still call her
    the WIDOW Olson?

    What was her first name, Jimmy?"

He thought along for two jackrabbits,
    and a half dozen chuckholes.
    "I d'know. We just called her the Widow Olson."

Then he told me about the next ranch
    a day's ride ahead.

The End

We've decided on cremation.

I don't want some undertaker
    lube job, change the oil,
    Budweiser propped between my feet
some first year cosmetician
    doing her Helene Rubenstein impersonations
    filling in my double chins
    with a trowel

some chauffeured limo stretching out for my pine box

and money I wouldn't spend on me alive
    counted out for my last "drop dead" outfit.

I'm going in a flash of flame
    so stack up some willow brush
    and if I go first
    save up my ashes in a jar
    mix 'em in with John's
    and toss us in the sage.

My last request is this:
Please don't let his next wife
    dump me in the chicken yard
    for my old hen's dust bath.

Storms Of Winter

Tempest wind, you
    whip
    iron chains
    across my back
    as lambs' wool frozen down
    warms the ice
    with dying,

    snow smothered calves
    curl into stone
    leave no scent
    for the cow to remember.
    She moans
    because no calf comes.

Wind sucks anger out of me
    where I can see it
    shake bare branches
    rough against the hawk's eye
    looking down.

    She grips branches
    that will sway with spring.

A Birth

Across the ditch
    she turns and stands
    as pain rolls down her side
    tail cast
    her nose drags a blur of snow and mud
    ignoring cows feeding past, calves stretched sleeping
I try not to intrude
    Some things are better left to reach their own point of
    brilliance
    even if they involve pain

But there is a tension
    a line deepening below her eye
There is a tightness
    in the twist of her lip
Even from this distance I can read
    the silence of her eyes

Once in the barn and tied
I seek to right the thing gone awry

Crimson scarves blow and swirl around my arm
    the heat surprising
    fingers gently probe a sacred place

Feet curled back
    the calf she wants to bear is blocked
I work between her pressing
    pushing back to give room
    to draw the legs forward, one at a time
Her body stiffens
    her eyes look beyond the present
    to a place of pain
    she has no reckoning of
    moments locked down on her

I clear the feet, then the pasterns
    a tip of black tongue curls
    licks my arm
    I sit down behind her
    brace my feet against her trembling legs
    we have a tug-of-war with this calf
    her great groan is muffled by mine
    there runs a red beading tear
    a crunching give
    and birth

Winter Night

It is nearing the break of night—
    shorter to dawn than the day that's been.
    Spring is an imagining.

I sculpt life from this
    ice mountain,
    chip slivers of day from the blue stillness.

Dreams softly touch earth
    without the weight of promise.

This night has no ending.
The clock turns its telling face.
I hold the owl's question up to the wind
    and let it blow away.

Nevada

This Nevada land
    is nothing—

    barren
    nothingness of desert
    only colors
    first and last

This raised lava flow
    fierce, ripped, writhing in place
    dusted with millions of years
    layer and layer of wind-blown, rain-carried, pulverized rock
    not even soil
    mere infinitesimal bits sifted up
    and on this
    aspen where snows bank
    quivering as a sage grouse drumming

    is nothing

Knobs and lines of distant hills
    ink dipped shading pale
    each form—its own perfection
    within my sight

    nothing

Breaks,
    short draws draining toward the Yellow Hills
    where stone-hard bones of Lahontan's fish
    Africa's elephant
    Arabia's camel
    Asia's redwood splintered on the sand—

    are nothing

Shard litter of weapons
    broken stone tools
    around me where I am seated in the enormity of this place
    Earth's heat warming me
    that warmed others forgotten years gone
    bewildered ones who found themselves born here
    roamed, camped, killed, birthed
    starved, sorrowed
    found God, rejoiced God

    all these nothing

Piddling spring
    that springs
    from the gravel bed
    beneath a rock face raising to a raven's nest
    flows—has always flowed—for miles—more
    knowing least resistance
    sustaining, sustaining

    nothing

That raven
    glistening black graceless bird
    flapping straight away
    watches time unfold

    and it is nothing

Shy creatures
    feed, fly
    scuttle, scare
    slither, slip
    haltingly step, arrogantly march
    thunder with conspicuous speed

    nothing

Sky in brightness
    opalized unearthly colors
    haughty, tauntingly stingy
    a fearsome boiling cauldron
    benevolent
    shadowed, calm
    translucent
    and in that great hollowness of night
    it becomes roan with stars
    expanding to source or destiny?

Silence
    the unshakable
    pierce
    of silence

    all nothing